THE
TWO-MINUTE
STORY
FOR NETWORK MARKETING

CREATE THE
BIG-PICTURE
STORY THAT
STICKS!

KEITH & TOM "BIG AL" SCHREITER

Published by Fortune Network Publishing
PO Box 890084
Houston, TX 77289 USA

Telephone: +1 (281) 280-9800

BigAlBooks.com

ISBN-13: 978-1-948197-15-1

ISBN-10: 1-948197-15-4

CONTENTS

BIG AL
WORKSHOPS

I travel the world 240+ days each year.
Let me know if you want me to stop in your
area and conduct a live Big Al training.

→ **BigAlSeminars.com** ←

FREE Big Al Training Audios
Magic Words for Prospecting

plus Free eBook and the Big Al Report!

→ **BigAlBooks.com/free** ←

PREFACE.

When master storyteller Jerry Scribner talks, people listen. This separates Jerry from everyone else. People hear what Jerry says. How does he do it?

Margaret Millar once said, "Most conversations are simply monologues delivered in the presence of a witness."

Sound familiar?

Does that remark apply to our presentations?

How many of our presentations have sounded like this?

1. We talked.

2. Our prospects listened.

And we did this for 20 minutes, 40 minutes, or even an hour. Brutal.

Oh, but we can make it worse. We can say to our prospects, "Please hold all your questions until the end. I might cover your questions later during my presentation."

Or, maybe we ask our prospects to sit in a hotel meeting room with other strangers while we show PowerPoint slides and videos for an hour.

No wonder prospects hate sales presentations.

The longer our presentation, the more we confuse prospects. There are just too many facts to remember.

To get decisions from prospects, we must be clear.

And that brings us back to Jerry Scribner. When Jerry talks, he simply tells a two-minute story about the most interesting subject in the world to prospects: themselves. This customized story has prospects sitting on the edge of their chairs, waiting to hear what comes next.

But the best part is that this two-minute story leads to a decision. This relieves prospects of the stress of feeling that they need more information, or that they need to think things over for days.

Here is a chance for us to change how we communicate with our prospects. In this book, we will learn how to use a short story to get our prospects to decide whether or not to join. No need for long presentations or sales props. This short story takes less than two minutes, while delivering precisely the information our prospects crave.

By capturing our prospects' total attention, we can now get our message from inside our heads, to inside our prospects' heads. This makes their decisions natural and easy.

Let's add the two-minute story to our inventory of great presentation methods we can use with our prospects.

THE PROBLEM.

After an hour and 30 minutes, the opportunity meeting finishes. John signs the application, buys his kit, and rushes home to build his business. This is going to be great!

When is the best time to start his business? The weekend, of course. No distractions. No job interfering with the day.

On Saturday morning John opens his distributor kit and reads the getting-started manual. Three coffees later, John feels exhausted. This is a lot of work. So much to learn, and so little time. Thankfully next weekend is free. That would be a great time to set his first appointment.

After seven days of begging, John's best friend agrees to meet him for a Saturday lunch. John shakes with excitement. All morning John practices his motivational exercises. He laminates his vision board, chants his affirmations, and sings his company song. Nothing can stop John. He has memorized his company presentation, word-for-word. His PowerPoint presentation is loaded in his new projector. This is going to be more than awesome.

At the restaurant, John's friend asks, "Why are you wearing a suit and tie?"

John replies, "I have this great business opportunity to show you. Let's clear off our restaurant table and set up our projector screen at the next table."

Things aren't feeling right for John's friend.

After only 25 minutes into the presentation, John's friend asks the waitress, "Is there a cliff nearby? I am looking for somewhere to jump."

One hour into the presentation, John's friend asks the waitress, "I want to fall on a sword. Would you hold a sword for me?"

Finally, John's friend passes out. Thankfully, that ends today's presentation.

As the medics haul John's friend out to the waiting ambulance, John thinks, "I need to set an appointment for next month. I wonder who I can talk to next?"

With one business presentation every month, how long do you think it will take John to build his business?

The answer?

Forever.

But, one little modification can change everything.

It's called the two-minute story.

THE BAD NEWS.

Among leaders, there is a joke. It goes like this:

There are two times when prospects are confused about our business opportunity.

1. Before we start our business presentation.

2. After we finish our business presentation.

Yes, our confusing presentations prevent our prospects from making "yes" decisions.

While we are talking about the wonderful company, the wonderful industry, the wonderful products, the wonderful training, and the wonderful compensation plan ... our prospects aren't listening.

What? Not listening to our great presentation about our wonderful opportunity?

How can this be?

Fact #1: Our prospect's attention span is short.

Fact #2: Our business presentation is 45 minutes.

Question: Can we figure out where things go wrong?

This is brutal.

We lose our prospects' attention at the first distraction. So, what are our prospects thinking while we give our rehearsed presentation?

"How long will this last?"

"Are you a salesman?"

"When are you going to get to the point?"

"How much is this going to cost?"

"Why did I allow this presentation to start?"

"How can I be sure I will be successful?"

"Why did I agree to this long sales pitch?"

"What would my friends think?"

"Probably all too good to be true."

"Who fed the dog tonight?"

"I could never memorize something this long."

"Will the babysitter charge me overtime?"

"I don't want to be a salesman."

"I have to wake up early for work tomorrow."

Yes, our prospects are not listening to us. Instead, they are having a conversation with themselves inside of their heads. We are a distraction to that conversation.

The solution?

We will solve this problem with our two-minute story presentation. This is a customized story for our prospects.

When our prospects hear their customized version of what could happen to them, they get excited. Why?

1. The story is about them. They are the most interesting people they know.

2. Because it is a story, they listen. We have programs in our minds that command us to listen to stories.

3. Their personal story commands them to make a decision to either learn a system and change their lives ... or keep their lives the same.

4. This story is not a win/lose or live/die presentation, but simply a way to explain what we do. The story is rejection-free. We don't know if right now is a good time or a bad time for our prospects. This story just lets our prospects know how our business works.

This is not a story that begins "Once upon a time," but a story of our prospects' possible future.

And what is even better?

This story talks to our prospects' subconscious minds in an easy, relaxed way. This allows our information to bypass their negativity, their too-good-to-be-true filters, their salesman alarms, skepticism, and dysfunctional programming. Nice!

Our story can actually transfer the message from our minds to our prospects' minds.

The two-minute story is magic.

My good friend Jerry Scribner is a master of the two-minute story and loves to use it. Why? Because his prospects love it, too.

Jerry sits down with a prospect over a cup of coffee. He tells the two-minute story ... and it is over. Done. Finished.

The prospect "gets it" right away. The rest of the coffee time can be for questions, enrolling online, or adding a couple of donuts.

Jerry has told the story so many times he doesn't even have to think about the words he uses. They are automatic. This allows him to spend 100% of his attention on his prospects. His prospects feel that connection too.

Seem too good to be true?

Read on, and see how we can simplify the decision for our prospects, and make it easy for them to say "yes" to our opportunity.

But first we have to address this.

Prospects avoid presentations. Why?

Presentations are too long. Presentations interfere with prospects' busy lives. Few prospects are naturally curious about our fact-filled sales pitches.

That is why prospects resist setting appointments to talk to us. It's time to fix that now.

WHY GETTING APPOINTMENTS FOR PRESENTATIONS IS HARD.

In 1960, there were no:

- cell phones.

- text messages.

- cable television channels.

- emails.

- social media streams.

If you asked someone, "Can I give you a 30-minute presentation about my new business opportunity?" ... they would reply:

"Woo-hoo! Entertainment!"

Because there wasn't anything to do in 1960.

But 1960 isn't coming back. Now prospects have a million things to keep them busy.

Today, life overwhelms prospects. So many activities, so many decisions, so many notifications that all scream, "Pay attention to me now!" Ugh.

Everyone is busy. They have to make choices every second about what they can pay attention to, and what they can ignore.

Our brains take in millions of bits of information every second. We have to be good to be at the top of all that information in our prospects' brains. We can't expect to stay at the top of our prospects' minds for 30 minutes. That would be superhuman.

If we try to give a 30-minute or 60-minute presentation today, ouch! Doing business today with ancient 1960 dinosaur techniques means that we will end up extinct, just like the dinosaurs.

We are swimming upstream. It's a losing battle.

What can we do?

For today's world, we need shorter options. One option is our book, *The One-Minute Presentation*. That is a simple and easy way for new networkers to begin their career. But it is only one option.

As we continue to grow as network marketers, so should our presentation skills. In this book we will explain how to do a more powerful presentation, the two-minute story technique.

Our presentations should be short.

Why?

1. Confidence. Our prospects will feel confident that they can duplicate a short presentation. They can visualize themselves talking to people in a concise, simple, and easy manner. They love that.

2. Easy to learn. No need to spend weeks practicing scripts or fumbling with boring PowerPoint slides. These presentations can be done anywhere.

3. No more fear of rejection. Short presentations sidestep rejection. Our prospects don't build up an impatient attitude and sales resistance when they know our presentation will be short.

4. Duplication. Our team members can duplicate simple skills such as:

   - Recommending and promoting things they like.

   - Using their own products or services.

   - Telling a two-minute story.

Team members will feel stressed if we ask them to do something too hard or out of their comfort zones. This is easy.

**Nothing happens unless we
have someone to talk to.**

Getting a willing audience for our presentation is the first step. Let's do that now.

The invitation breakdown.

All of the words in the two-minute story work hard. Amateurs talk to prospects with whatever words come to mind. Verbal diarrhea is not an effective approach for network marketing professionals. We need to do better.

We should study the words in our two-minute story and see how and why they work.

Does this mean we can't change these words? Of course not. But before we adjust our two-minute story for our personal use, we should know what these words accomplish.

Here are the first words we will use to get a willing audience for our two-minute story.

"I've got a good story..."

Five words.

Magic.

With these five words we can get unlimited presentations. Prospects can't resist these five words. Let's see what they do.

What good does it do to give a presentation when no one is listening? Before we start any presentation, we want to:

1. Get permission from our prospects.

2. Have our prospects' attention.

How will we get our prospects' attention? With words, of course. We carefully choose these words, "I've got a good story." These words get a specific reaction from our prospects. We get their immediate attention.

Stories are powerful. The best way for humans to learn and predict the future? Stories. Our internal programs tell us to listen to stories. Why? Because stories help us know what to do in the future so that we survive. The short story is, we can't resist a story.

Imagine that we are walking past three people at work. One person is telling a story. What does our subconscious mind command us to do? Stop. Listen to the story. Our subconscious mind has a program that says:

"If anyone, anywhere, at any time, is telling a story, we must stop and listen to the story all the way to the end. We cannot go on in life unless we know how the story ends."

Yes, stories are riveting. We love stories. That is why we like movies, books, and Hollywood gossip.

As soon as children can speak, they will say, "Mommy, Daddy, please tell me a story."

These powerful words, "I've got a good story," guarantee that our prospects will pay attention.

Notice our choice of words. We said, "I've got a good story."

We did not say, "I've got a good sales presentation."

See the difference? Our choice of words is critical.

"Takes about two minutes."

Not all stories are worth listening to. Especially if they take a long time. Our listeners guard their time. Too many things to do, and too little time.

Because we are polite, we will promise that our story will be short. When we say, "Takes about two minutes," how do our prospects feel?

They feel great. They want to hear our story. They relax when they know it will be short.

What else happens? Because we promise a short story, our prospects want to hear our story immediately. No need for follow-up or getting back to prospects later. Isn't it great when prospects want to hear what we have to say? No more rejection for us.

"Might make you a lot of money ..."

These words announce to our prospects that we are giving a commercial message. This is about business. Now, think about this from our prospects' point of view.

Do prospects like money? Yes. Already our story is interesting.

But the best part is that our prospects won't set up their sales defenses. It is a story. Not a sales presentation. They can listen safely to our story. This is important. If our prospects have their salesman alarms going off, they will be skeptical and resistant to everything we say.

"… might not."

We started our sentence by saying, "Might make you a lot of money…"

Just to make sure that we don't set off any salesman alarms, we soften our commercial message by adding, "might not." Now we can be sure that our prospects can relax.

So, the complete sentence is, "Might make you a lot of money, might not."

Our prospects think, "Make a lot of money? Yes! Might not? Oh, that seems fair. No need to worry about some hard-selling sales presentation by a pushy salesman."

Our prospects are thinking this using their conscious minds. But do we really care about our prospects' conscious minds? No. What did we learn from our books on closing? We learned that decisions by our prospects are made in their subconscious minds, the automatic part of their brains.

The survival program rules our subconscious minds. It says, "We have to live. We have to survive." This is a good program to have. It protects us from dangerous situations. This is also the program that alerts us to salespeople. It tells us to be cautious when someone is asking for our money. We need money to survive.

So, the real question is, "What are our prospects thinking in their subconscious minds?"

When our prospects' subconscious minds hear, "Might make you a lot of money," here is how their subconscious minds react:

"Money? We need money! We need money for food, shelter, clothing. We need money to survive. Yes!"

But it is the second half of the sentence that really sells our prospects. When our prospects' subconscious minds hear, "Might not," their subconscious minds panic. Their subconscious minds react like this:

"Oh no! What do you mean might not? We need money to survive. We need food, shelter and clothing! We have to get that money. We will look for reasons why this will work for us, instead of reasons why it will not."

Wow. This puts our prospects in a positive frame of mind. They are excited about the possibilities of our story. No skepticism. Our prospects now look for reasons to make our story work. It doesn't get much better than this.

"Want to hear it?"

This little question checks to see if our prospects still want to hear our story. What do you think prospects will say?

"Yes." They can't wait to hear our story. We love asking questions when we already know the answer. We have permission from our prospects to tell our story. We have permission for two minutes of our prospects' time.

Good news. Our story will take much less than two minutes. They will be impressed.

Let's review these words.

When we put these words together, it looks like this:

"I've got a good story. Takes about two minutes. Might make you a lot of money, might not. Want to hear it?"

Now we see these words in a new light. By using carefully-chosen words, we get predictable results. Our prospects desperately want to hear our story.

Let's ask ourselves, "If we said these words three times a day, how many people would want to hear our story?"

The answer is, "Three."

It is easy to give three presentations every day. Since our two-minute story will be a short presentation, we can fit our business into even the busiest of schedules. Think of how many two-minute story presentations we could give during coffee break, lunch, or on the phone on the way home.

Here is another question.

"What if everyone on our team gave three business presentations every day?"

The answer? "Wow."

Why doesn't our team give more presentations?

Maybe because we did not tell them exactly what to say to get presentations. Now we know what to say.

Let's do the math.

Three two-minute story presentations a day, 30 days a month, means 90 prospects heard our two-minute story presentation. That is more than enough presentations to create momentum and excitement in our groups.

Now, let's learn the words for our two-minute story presentation and why they work.

OUR TWO-MINUTE STORY BEGINS.

Our prospect is waiting. We will start with a question to get our prospects even more engaged.

"Would it be okay if you never had to go to work again?"

This question does some heavy lifting in our presentation.

Network marketers ask, "How do I guess my prospects' motivation? How do I create the perfect vision in their minds? What if I assume they want one thing, but it turns out I was wrong?"

This is a serious question. However, the solution is easy. Our prospects may not openly tell us their motivation for looking at our business, but we don't have to guess. We can command our prospects' subconscious minds to instantly give our prospects their motivation.

Magic happens when we ask, "Would it be okay if you never had to go to work again?" Our prospect's subconscious mind reacts and instantly flashes the most important motivation to the prospect.

If we said this phrase to five prospects, each prospect would instantly have a different vision. Some examples:

1. Waking up at noon because they are a night person.

2. Walking around in their pajamas all day long.

3. Home-schooling the children and taking unlimited long weekends.

4. Golfing during the week when the golf courses are empty.

5. Fulfilling their life-long dream of playing the guitar and writing music.

We won't have to guess our prospects' motivation. Our prospects will automatically know what is right for them. What we ask them to do is to imagine what it would be like if they never had to go to work again. Their vision excites them. They love the dream.

Why are we so sure that our prospects will create the perfect vision in their minds?

Because we commanded it. We start our question with the words, "Would it be okay if ..."

These words are powerful. When we say these words, our prospects naturally go along with our suggestion. We don't want to take any chances, so that is why we use these words.

A little history into the phrase, "Would it be okay if ...?"

When we say this, the subconscious mind of our prospect thinks, "Oh, that is polite. Of course I will go along with what you say, as long as it is reasonable." This reaction is automatic.

You can feel how quickly the "yes" decision pops up when I ask the following questions:

"Would it be okay if you held the door for me?"

"Would it be okay if we let her join us?"

"Would it be okay if we sit over here?"

"Would it be okay if I started now?"

Do we feel the automatic agreement?

Now, what do you think happens in our prospects' minds when we say, "Would it be okay if you never had to go to work again?"

They visualize what this would mean to them. Now they have their vision of what life could be if they didn't have to go to their jobs. Exciting!

Then we pause for just a bit, so our prospects have a chance to experience their personal vision in their minds.

Then, we will continue with this question.

"So how much money would you need a month, just to cover the basic bills, so that you would never have to show up at work?"

Please notice that we did not ask our prospects how much money they earned. That is too personal and invasive. Prospects would hesitate to give us that information anyway. But all we ask is the minimum amount they need monthly to take care of their bills.

We have a strategy for this. We want to keep this figure as low as possible. What if we asked, "How much money would you like to earn?"

Our prospects might reply with billions of dollars a month. We can't meet that expectation with our business.

The smaller our prospects' initial goals, the easier it will be for our business to meet those goals.

Our prospects might answer, "Well, if I did not have to go to work, my expenses would be much lower. We wouldn't need that second car and the extra insurance. Plus, no more childcare expenses. So, if I could stay home, the minimum amount I would need to cover all of our bills and some pizza delivery charges would be $5,000 a month."

Now, this would be a great answer. However, sometimes our prospects aren't clear, and we might have to explain that we are looking for just the minimum expenses for now.

Remember this number.

We will use this important number later in our presentation. When we know how much our prospect needs monthly, we can better explain exactly which activities will create that income. Our presentation will be customized to exactly what our prospect wants and needs.

Narrowing the decision-making funnel.

This may not be clear now, but it will be later. We need the minimum amount our prospect requires to never show up for work again. It is the beginning of our narrowing of the decision-making funnel.

Here is what happens in an old-school presentation. Prospects get overloaded with information. Too much information, too many decisions to make. Our prospects might be thinking, "I don't know if the products will sell. What do they mean in the compensation plan explanation about non-competing volume? I didn't understand everything

about the products, so how can I be sure if I can sell them? And when they use words such as sponsoring, recruiting, downline, upline, and personal volume, what does that really mean? Maybe I need to do more research first."

If our prospects are thinking this at the end of our presentation, ouch. And then we say, "Okay, make up your mind now."

That is pretty unfair, isn't it? We asked our prospects to make a final decision when there are so many questions and lots of confusion in their minds. That is ugly. We know that confused minds always say, "No."

So, we intend to build a funnel that helps our prospects go down a simple path. At the end of the path, they will only have to make one decision.

This is easier and kinder to our prospects.

We will continue to build this decision-making funnel as we continue our story.

Information collecting: Done!

What's next? Now we must describe our business in a way that our prospects can comfortably understand.

The big mistake would be to describe our business in the way **we** understand. Our prospects haven't attended the same meetings and trainings that we have. They don't understand our special language of PV, BV, legs, bonuses, etc. So, we will talk in our prospects' language.

Let's review.

The invitation and first sentences of our two-minute story are easy, with no rejection.

"I've got a good story. Takes about two minutes. Might make you a lot of money, might not. Want to hear it?"

"Would it be okay if you never had to go to work again?"

"So how much money would you need a month, just to cover the basic bills, so that you would never have to show up at work?"

A lot happens in these first sentences, and our prospects want more. Why? Because the story is all about them.

And now, the real magic begins.

Onward to our next sentences!

THE SECRET QUESTION OUR PROSPECTS DON'T KNOW HOW TO ASK.

When presenting our business to prospects, what is their biggest question or concern about our products or services?

Here are some possibilities:

1. How good is the quality of the products or services?

2. What are the test results of the products or services?

3. How much do the products or services cost?

4. How fast is delivery?

5. Is there a guarantee?

These are great questions.

But our prospects have a bigger question they need to have answered. They never ask this question. But if we don't answer this question, they will hesitate to join.

What is the big secret question our prospects don't know how to ask?

"If I get involved with your business, will anyone buy these products and services?"

Sure, our products and services may be great, but will people buy them? Or do we have great products and services that no one buys?

If we represent the world's greatest product, but no one buys it, how will our business look? It will look broke. Then our prospects' friends will ridicule them for making a bad decision.

How do we assure our prospects that our products and services are in demand?

One way to address this is to tell prospects about our successful retailing experiences. We could mention the times when prospects approached us, instead of us approaching them. That is what our prospects want to know.

We could say:

"I take my can of diet powder to work with me every day. I enjoy the low calorie mini-meal instead of the donut during coffee break. Last week three co-workers came over to my desk and asked about the diet powder and I sold 6 cans!"

That wasn't hard. And our prospect's question is answered. Here are a few other examples:

"After I helped my neighbor save money on his electric bill, three more neighbors asked me if I could do the same for them."

"When I got back from my discounted cruise, many of my co-workers asked me to get them discounted cruises also."

"After using this wrinkle-reducer for 30 days, my skeptical sister said she wanted it too. And then she told three of her friends about it. They ordered immediately."

"The package delivery driver said he loved how my house smelled. When I told him I am using all-natural cleaners now, he wanted to order some for his house too."

"When I shared that now I sleep great at night, everyone at the club wanted to know what I was taking."

Spend time answering the right question.

Quality, delivery, guarantee, ingredients ... these are things our prospects might have questions about. But as professionals, we have to be responsible and answer the secret question in their minds. We have to let our prospects know that there is a willing market of prospects who will buy our products and services.

There is another way to answer our prospect's secret question.

We will use this second way of answering this question for our two-minute story presentation.

How else can we assure the prospect there is a willing market for our products and services? By commanding our prospects to believe it.

Yes, we will use a special phrase that makes it easy for our prospect to believe our message. Here is the magic phrase.

"Well, you know how ..."

When we say the phrase, "Well, you know how," our prospect immediately thinks:

"Well, if I already know how, then it must be true. Why? Because what I know is true. No further proof needed. No testimonials. No research reports. No documentation."

Yes, we actually command our prospect to believe what we are going to say next. Starting with this phrase makes it easy for us to get our prospect's agreement. This saves time for both of us.

After we say the phrase, "Well, you know how," we will simply tell our prospects that our products are in demand. Now they don't have to worry.

How does this sound in real life?

Here are a few ideas.

"Well, you know how people are always taking vitamins?" Our prospects nod in agreement. They now believe there is a market for vitamins.

"Well, you know how everyone gets an electricity bill?" Our prospects feel that there would be a large market for our electricity services.

"Well, you know how people hate wrinkles?" Now we've established that there is a market for our anti-wrinkle creams.

"Well, you know how travel is so expensive?" This means there is a huge market for discounted travel, because of course people want to save money.

"Well, you know how people buy a lot of energy drinks?" Our prospects will think, "Wow. People do buy a lot of energy drinks. If your business sells energy drinks, there is a huge market for them."

"Well, you know how people are always dieting and trying to lose a few pounds?" This means there is a huge market for our diet products.

Commanding is a shortcut.

We command our prospects to believe there is a market by starting with the words, "Well, you know how ..."

This saves everyone's time. They understand there is a market for our products. We can move forward and keep the story short and interesting.

Now we can move to the next sentence of our two-minute story presentation.

LET'S GET TO THE POINT.

Prospects don't want to hear about our company. Well, at least not now. Later, if they decide to join, they will want to know more company details. But for now, they just want us to get to the point of our story.

We need to make this short. We can't drone on endlessly about the company founders, the history of the company, patents and trademarks, awards won, etc. This isn't a question in the minds of our prospects right now. What do our prospects want to know?

Not much.

Our prospects already know that there is a demand for our products and services. There is no need to sell them on the company at this moment. So we will make this section short, and maybe make a tiny sales plug.

How would that sound? Like this:

"Well, there is a company called the Wonderful Company, and they have lots of customers who rave about their products."

Now, this is very generic. Why? Because this part of our two-minute story will be different for everyone, depending on their companies. So let's give examples of how this would sound when combined with the previous sentence we learned in the last chapter.

"Well, you know people are always taking vitamins? There is a company called the Wonderful Company that produces vitamins that you can feel making a difference."

"Well, you know how everyone gets an electricity bill? There is a company called the Wonderful Company that helps people get a lower bill."

"Well, you know how people hate wrinkles? There is a company called the Wonderful Company that makes an anti-wrinkle cream that women rave about."

"Well, you know how travel is so expensive? There is a company called the Wonderful Company that will allow you to be a part-time travel agent. Then, you can travel at wholesale prices."

"Well, you know how people buy a lot of energy drinks? There is a company called the Wonderful Company that makes an all-natural energy drink that tastes even better than those unhealthy ones."

"Well, you know how people are always dieting and trying to lose a few pounds? There is a company called the Wonderful Company that helps people lose weight naturally, just by drinking their special breakfast shake."

Is that it?

Yes, that's it. The company's credibility and stability might come up later, but it is not an issue now. Right now, our prospects only want to hear the end of the story.

Let's review.

Our two-minute story invitation was short. It only took a few seconds. Here it is again:

"I've got a good story. Takes about two minutes. Might make you a lot of money, might not. Want to hear it?"

This didn't take long, and it is very effective.

But what about our two-minute story presentation?

Now, we are four sentences into our actual two-minute story. What have we done with our four sentences?

1. We got our prospects to dream.

2. Our prospects told us how much money they need so they would not have to show up for work again.

3. We explained to our prospects the wonderful products and services that we represent.

4. Now our prospects are thinking, "Yeah, they are probably a pretty good company with some pretty good products and services."

So let's see how these four sentences would look like in real life. Here is an example:

The story.

"Would it be okay if you never had to go to work again?

"So how much money would you need a month, just to cover the basic bills, so that you would never have to show up at work?

"Well, you know how everyone gets an electricity bill?

"There is a company called the Wonderful Company that helps people get a lower bill."

That was quick and easy. All four sentences did the job.

Let's do a few more examples.

"Would it be okay if you never had to go to work again?

"So how much money would you need a month, just to cover the basic bills, so that you would never have to show up at work?

"Well, you know how people are always dieting and trying to lose a few pounds?

"There is a company called the Wonderful Company that helps people lose weight naturally, just by drinking their special breakfast shake."

"Would it be okay if you never had to go to work again?

"So how much money would you need a month, just to cover the basic bills, so that you would never have to show up at work?

"Well, you know how people are so concerned about the environment nowadays?

"There is a company called the Wonderful Company that makes all-natural cleaning products that people can now use in their homes."

"Would it be okay if you never had to go to work again?

"So how much money would you need a month, just to cover the basic bills, so that you would never have to show up at work?

"Well, you know how women spend a fortune to delay their wrinkles?

"There is a company called the Wonderful Company that developed a wrinkle reducer that works in just 60 seconds."

"Would it be okay if you never had to go to work again?

"So how much money would you need a month, just to cover the basic bills, so that you would never have to show up at work?

"Well, you know how everyone gets a telephone wireless bill every month?

"There is a company called the Wonderful Company that teaches people how to cut their wireless bill by 25%, 50%, or even get their service free."

Okay, that was fast.

We are four sentences into our story. How long did it take?

About 25 seconds!

We are moving fast and things are about to get serious and interesting.

The first four sentences of our two-minute story are the basics.

The real magic?

The exciting part starts with the next sentence. The next four sentences are complicated and do the heavy work. Let's begin.

THE SECOND HALF OF OUR TWO-MINUTE STORY BEGINS.

Now, we have to deliver. Our prospects told us how much money they need every month so they would never have to go to work again. We have to show our prospects a plan to achieve that.

The second half of our two-minute story will do that. Our prospects' interest in our story is high.

The next sentence.

This sentence is long and complicated. Plus, we will customize this sentence to our business opportunity. To make things simpler in this book, we will use one company example for now. We will imagine that we sold diet products for the next four sentences.

Here is the example sentence, and then we will break down what is really happening. Remember, this example sentence is for diet products only.

"Now, if you wanted to never go to work again, all you would have to do is eventually locate 125 people who wanted to lose weight one time, and keep it off forever, by changing what they have for breakfast."

What???

Oh, a lot happened here. Let's break it down.

First, we started with the word, "Now." Why? We need our prospects' attention. Our prospects' minds are still thinking about our previous sentences. We have to stop those thoughts.

What do we want our prospects to be thinking about? We want to remind them of the purpose of our story. We want them to mentally experience the feeling of never having to go to work again. By saying the word, "Now," it shocks them into stopping their current thoughts and paying attention to our next words.

Then what are our next words? "If you wanted to never go to work again."

At this point we have the total attention of our prospects. Our prospects are thinking about the experience of never going to work again. They want to know how this could happen. Our prospects are on the edge of their seats.

Next, we use the words, "All you would have to do is."

What would this mean to our prospects? These words trigger a feeling inside of our prospects' minds. They think, "This sounds like it is going to be easy. Or, at least simple to understand." Our prospects feel positive about our next words. This moves the story along quickly in their minds. They love that we are getting to the point.

How do we explain our business?

If we talked to one hundred network marketing distributors, 95 of them could not explain the details of how their company's compensation plan works. Well, if distributors don't know, how could we expect our prospects to understand in 15 or 20 seconds? Impossible!

Plus, our prospects don't want to know the compensation plan now. The compensation plan is only interesting after they make a decision to join. Let's be kind to our prospects and talk to them about what they want to know. After all, this is **their** story, isn't it?

What do our prospects want to know about our business? At this point in their decision-making process, not much. They want the big picture.

Generally, their thoughts are, "What would I have to do? Do I have to get my PhD in nutrition? Will I have to spend millions in advertising? Will I have to rent office space and be liable for leases? How many employees will I need? Do I have to knock on my neighbor's doors and beg for sales? Do I have to go back to school?"

We can eliminate this thinking with a simple explanation. We will tell them exactly what they would have to do to earn enough money to never have to go to work again. This should bring a sigh of relief to our prospects.

All the details about the company background, the research, the patents, the longevity, etc., can be saved for later. If our prospects are not interested, there is no need for them to know this information. If they are interested and want to join, they will ask for this information. But that happens after our two-minute story presentation.

The tricky part is learning how to simplify our business in terms that our prospects understand. They want this explanation in seconds.

Do our prospects understand network marketing? Do they understand levels, sponsoring, legs, and matching bonuses?

No. We cannot use these words, and we cannot talk about these things now. This is not how ordinary prospects see the world. Yes, there will be exceptions. But even with the exceptions, they want most of the data much later, after they make a decision to join.

How do ordinary prospects see business?

In the simplest terms, our prospects see business in terms of customers. In their minds, they have a vision of a business owner at a checkout counter in a small store. Our prospects understand customers buying or using products and services. If more customers come into our store, we earn more money. If fewer customers come into our store, we earn less money.

So, let's talk to our prospects in terms that they understand. We will talk about customers. And, we will combine the usage of distributors and customers into our simplified totals. (Don't panic. There is another way, but we will cover that later.)

For now, we will forget about the features and benefits of our compensation plan and the history of our company.

We will talk about the happy customers of our products and services.

And now comes the mathematics.

Remember the second sentence of our two-minute story? We asked our prospects how much money they would need so that they would never have to show up for work again.

In our example, our prospects told us $5,000 a month. Naturally our prospects would like to know what they would have to do to earn that money.

We will give them the big-picture overview and make it simple for them to understad. If our explanation is too complicated and difficult, our prospects will go into research and contemplation mode. Then, they might never get back to us again.

Simple. That is the most important word for us to remember right now. Simple.

In our diet products example, how many users (customers and distributors) would we need to earn $5,000 a month? That is all the mathematics that we need to know.

Now you might be thinking, "Well, that depends. Are all the customers my personal customers? What if 25% of those customers are on level 3? Or, it would depend on my current rank at the time."

Yes, we could create hundreds of scenarios and organization structures and come up with hundreds of different answers. This is not the time for that. This is the time to be simple.

We will make a rough, average estimation. Yes, we can manipulate the data to make the number of customers go up or down. However, that is not what our prospects want to know now. They want to know, "Generally, what do I have to do?"

So to make it simple for our prospects, we will give them one scenario. Later we can discuss how to manipulate the numbers of customers needed up or down depending on organizational structure, etc.

Here is what we tell our prospects.

"Now, if you wanted to never go to work again, all you would have to do is eventually locate 125 people who wanted to lose weight one time, and keep it off forever, by changing what they have for breakfast."

How did we get to 125 people? We used some simple mathematics.

We estimated that the average retail and bonus profit for a retail customer was $40. If we wanted to earn $5,000 a month, we would need 125 customers.

We could have figured the profit per customer at $1, $10, or even $100. This depends on our products and services, and how we want to customize our presentation. But for the purposes of this initial example, we used $40 for a diet products customer.

This is simple for our prospects to understand. If they want $5,000, they have to accumulate 125 people who want to lose weight one time, and keep it off forever, by changing what they eat for breakfast. Later, if they decide to join our business, we can discuss other scenarios.

But forget about what we think at the moment. What is important is what our prospects think.

Our prospects are gasping for oxygen.

When our prospects hear they have to find 125 customers, they panic.

They think, "I don't know 125 people. Oh, this is way too hard. I am not a salesman. Who would I talk to? This is impossible!"

Relax.

This is what anyone would think.

We will handle their negative feelings in the next sentence. And don't worry. It is okay for our prospects to have this moment of fear.

Back to our prospects.

Let's look inside the minds of our prospects and see what they are thinking. Perhaps they are thinking:

"I felt excited about never going to work again. You said it was going to be simple. Well, maybe simple for you, but impossible for me. While I would love to never go to work again, I can't envision myself getting 125 customers. I feel depression taking over again. I was hoping to leave my job."

Well, we did explain exactly what our prospects had to do. Our explanation was clear.

We will help our prospects recover in the next sentence of our story.

But for now, let's apply this simplicity to some other examples.

More examples of what prospects would have to do.

We will customize this one-sentence explanation to include our products and services. Remember, our prospects think in terms of "customers buying stuff," and it is too early for them to understand our compensation plan. Also, remember that we will generally describe what they would have to do. Our prospects want the overview now. Details will come later if they want to join.

Here are some examples:

"All you would have to do is get 10 ladies a month to change their skincare program to our premium brand that fights the wrinkles they hate. And then, after just one year, you would earn an extra $5,000 a month."

"All you have to do is give out our premier vitamin sample packs to people who currently take vitamins. Most people will continue to use their current vitamins, but some will love how our vitamins make them feel, and become lifelong customers. Eventually you will have 200 people ordering their vitamins from you. And then you would earn an extra $5,000 a month."

"All you would have to do is between you, and everybody you know, and everybody they talk to, forever and ever and ever, is eventually accumulate 250 people who want chemicals out of their homes, and natural products in. And then you would earn an extra $5,000 a month."

(This wording makes it a bit easier for prospects to understand large numbers of customers. They will see that they don't have to talk to everyone personally.)

"All you would have to do is find 20 responsible people who want to work part-time, and want to earn money by helping their neighbors save money on their utility bills. You will teach them how to get new customers weekly, and how to be consistent in their part-time work. And then you would earn an extra $5,000 a month."

(If the commissions from individual customers are small, we could give this simplified explanation. We would describe how many good distributors working part-time they would need to produce a large number of customers.)

"All you would have to do is find people who love to travel frequently, and who would love to pay less for their packaged holidays. You will need to accumulate 120 frequent travelers. And then you would earn an extra $5,000 a month."

"All you would have is eventually get 200 families who care about the environment to change their regular cleaning products to natural products. And then you would earn an extra $5,000 a month."

"All you would have to do is find 500 people who want their phone bills to be lower, and help them start getting their smaller bills from us. And then you would earn an extra $5,000 a month."

"But this isn't the whole story. They need to know more!"

Yes, this isn't the whole story. But this is not the time for the gritty details, disclaimers, compensation models, and explanations of the precise procedures of getting these customers. That will come later if our prospects want to know more. For now, they just want to know, "Generally, what do I have to do?"

Our prospects want to know if it is something that is doable. Does it require special skills? Is it something that would be too uncomfortable for them?

Our two-minute story is about our prospects, not about our business. We have to focus on what our prospects want at this time.

So where are we now?

Our prospects felt excited about a new career. We crushed their dreams by telling them they had to get hundreds of customers. Our prospects think, "Oh my. I had dreams of an early retirement. Traveling the world. Following my passions. But, I don't know that many people. Plus, I am shy and don't know what to say. I don't know how to get that many people so I can realize my dreams."

And here we come to the rescue.

In our next sentence, we are going to make our prospects feel much better. We will do a cool mind-reading trick to gain their trust first.

Our prospects recover.

In the last chapter, we left our customers depressed with little hope of getting hundreds of customers. Their thoughts were concentrated on this problem. But that is not where we want their thoughts. We have to regain their attention. Again, we will use the word "now" to break their train of thought.

Here are the next sentences. Many things happen within the sentences, but don't worry. We will break down the sentences into the important parts and explain why they work. We'll continue, using the diet products example.

The next sentences.

"Now, you don't know how to get 125 customers, but you can learn. You learned how to use a smartphone, you learned how to drive a car, and you certainly can learn a system to get 125 customers to change what they eat for breakfast."

Let's see why this works.

"Now" gets our prospects' attention and refocuses them back on our conversation. We cannot have our prospects thinking in the past. We need their total attention.

"You don't know how to get 125 customers."

Yes, we successfully read their minds. That was exactly what they were thinking. Our prospects respond by thinking, "Wow! You read my mind. I was feeling depressed, but you understand. You know how desperate I feel. I would like to get 125 customers, but I don't know how. Finally, someone who understands me."

"But, you can learn."

What do our prospects think now?

"Learn? Well, I am not sure. I tried learning in high school, and it was hard. I have some doubts."

We don't want to make a mistake here. Yes, we can tell them that they can learn, but they have to believe it. We don't want to continue until our prospects totally believe that they could learn a new skill. What is the easiest way to create that belief?

We will remind our prospects of successful learning experiences in the past. After one experience, their minds will think, "Yes, it is possible."

But we will go further. We will give them another example. After two successful examples of learning new things, our prospects will think, "Of course I can learn. I successfully learned many things in the past."

All we have to do is to pick successful learning experiences from our prospects' past. Let's be professional and pick learning experiences that our prospects can relate to. Here are some examples.

"You learned how to use a smartphone, you learned how to drive a car."

Great example for most people, but not all. What if our prospect doesn't drive a car? Then we could say this:

"You learned how to use the remote control on your television, and you learned how to dance."

Great for prospects who watch television and know how to dance. But maybe a prospect might be dance-impaired. Then we could say this:

"You learned how to do your current job, and you learned how to get home every night after work."

Let's continue.

At this point our prospects believe they can learn new things. We took the extra time to make sure that they have this belief. Without this belief, the rest of the sentence is weak. We need their ironclad belief to move on.

"And you certainly."

It doesn't take a rocket scientist to see that these words give our prospects the belief that what we will say next will be true. At this point our prospects should be mentally recovering with the assurances that they can learn new things.

"Can learn a system."

"System" brings up many thoughts in our prospects' minds. Prospects love systems. They believe that systems work. And at first, they have a question in the back of their minds when they look at an opportunity. Their question is, "Is there a system that would make this work ... if I just followed the system?"

The McDonald's franchise is well-known for its system. Any 16-year-old can step into the system, follow the directions, and make a hamburger. Armies recruit 18-year-olds to fly multimillion-dollar jets. Armies use a system. Our prospects can see themselves reading a system manual and learning exactly how to do something new. They believe they can learn new things (thanks to us), so this will bring a smile to their faces.

Does your company have a system? Of course it does. Our prospects will have training available from the company, our upline, and of course, from us. Our system may be formal or informal, but we have a system to get the results we need.

Remember the word "system," as we will use this in the next chapter to answer objections. For example, our prospects might say, "But I don't know anyone."

Our response will be, "Of course you don't know anyone. Our system will show you how to get all the prospects you need."

Our opportunity is getting easier for the prospect to understand and believe.

We'll talk more about systems in the next chapter.

MANAGING OUR PROSPECTS' DECISIONS.

Earlier we discussed "managing the decision-making funnel." We talked about how ordinary presentations have too many unanswered questions. We use the word "system" to manage this funnel. We can answer any questions our prospects have with, "You will learn that in our system."

New distributors don't have all the answers to every question, so this is great for them. But this answer is also awesome for prospects.

Here are some quick examples.

Prospects: "I don't know where to find people who want to lose weight."

Us: "Don't worry. You will learn how to do that in the system."

Prospects: "I don't know how to talk to people like a salesman."

Us: "Don't worry. You will learn how to talk to people easily when you learn our system."

Prospects: "I am not comfortable talking to strangers."

Us: "Don't worry. You will learn how to be very comfortable when you learn our system."

Prospects: "I don't know how to do this or any business."

Us: "Don't worry. The company doesn't expect you to know how to do our business before you start. That is why we have training. You will learn how to do this business step-by-step when you learn our system."

We will answer our prospects' questions by referring to the "system." This will give our prospects confidence that they can successfully build their business.

But back to managing the decision funnel for our prospects.

It is unfair to ask prospects to make a final decision when they have lots of unanswered questions. Almost every question in our prospects' minds can be answered with, "You will learn it in our system."

We want to make our prospect's decision easy.

How?

Our prospects don't have to worry about questions such as:

- "Can I do this business?"

- "What if there is something I don't know how to do?"

- "Will this be too hard for me to learn?"

- "What if I don't have the right contacts?"

- "How can I be sure that I will be able to do this?"

We answer all of these questions by telling our prospects they will learn these things in our system.

Our system handles everything!

Now our prospects only have one question.

If our system answers all of their concerns about being able to do our business, only one question remains.

"Do I want to learn this system so that I have a business that can change my life?"

That's it.

We removed all the extraneous questions and distractions from our prospects' minds. Now all they have to consider is if they want to learn our system and change their lives … or not.

This is a much kinder way to present to prospects. They don't have to be stressed about multiple unknown factors and the risk of making a bad decision. Prospects love a simple explanation that makes their decisions easy.

And finally, just one more reminder.

Early in our presentation, we explained exactly which activities our prospects had to do to earn an extra $5,000 a month. We assured our prospects they could learn a system. So now we wrap up our presentation with these final words:

"And then you would earn an extra $5,000 a month."

Yes, we should remind our prospects of our earlier promise. This completes our presentation, so now it is time for our prospects to make their final decision.

Nine proven words.

In the previous chapter, we managed our prospects' decision-making funnels. We won't torture prospects by asking them to make decisions with so many unanswered questions in their minds.

Instead, we narrowed our prospects' decision to:

1. Continue their lives as is …

or,

2. Join our business and learn a system.

These are two very clear choices.

This makes it easy for our prospects to make a quick final decision.

We will use special words to prompt our prospects to make this decision, stress-free.

No more brutal staring at each other, uncomfortable silences or high-pressure closing techniques. Instead, we will ask a natural question that is easy and fair for our prospects to answer. Here is the question:

"So what is going to be easier for you?"

That's it. Nine words. Now, before we give our prospects the two choices, let's talk about these nine proven words.

How do our prospects feel when they hear these words? Here are some of their thoughts:

"Sounds like I am going to have some choices. This is great. This is not some salesman trying to push me into a corner. I can decide what I want."

"I love people who give me choices. I like having additional options in my life."

"Wow. This person wants what will be easier for me. This person has my best interests at heart. No agenda. I feel like giving this person a giant hug."

"Well, let me choose what is easier. And when I choose what is easier, that means I won't have to think this over. I can make my decision now."

"I am no fool. I am programmed to do what is easier, not harder. Of course I want to do what is easier for me."

Prospects love hearing these nine words. This means our presentation is over. It was short. Barely longer than a minute. Certainly less than two minutes. And, our prospects don't have to deal with some pushy salesperson. Our prospects can make their choices and relax. Our prospects already know if our opportunity will serve them or not.

Now, let's get busy and give our prospects their choices.

Two choices.

We say to our prospects, "So what is going to be easier for you?" Then, we immediately give our prospects these two choices.

1. Continue their lives as is …

or,

2. Join our business and learn a system.

That's it.

The choices are easy. We don't stress our prospects. We make sure the choice is clear.

Does it matter which choice we give them first? No. We froze our prospects' minds when we said those nine words. We have their total attention. Don't worry about which choice we give our prospects first. We can say what feels natural for us.

Let's investigate those two choices.

#1. Keep their current life as it is.

We respect the decision that our prospects may want to stay exactly where they are. It is certainly an option for them. They don't have to change. They know this anyway, so let's bring it out into the open. They will feel good that we respectfully acknowledge that not changing is an option for them.

What we say next will change depending on each prospect's current situation. Why? Because all of our prospects currently have different situations in their lives. For some prospects, we can describe keeping their situation as struggling with one paycheck. For other prospects, we can describe the dissatisfaction of working for a rude boss.

#2. Our solution, which is to learn a system that will change their lives.

This gives us a chance to remind our prospects of the benefits of learning a simple system for our business.

Remember, we are reducing the decision for our prospects to learning a system or not. No other choices.

Here are some starter examples.

"So what is going to be easier for you? To continue commuting one hour each way to work for the rest of your life? Or, learning a system to get 125 customers who want to lose weight by changing what they have for breakfast?"

A very simple choice. Let's try some more examples.

"So what is going to be easier for you? To continue placing the children in daycare, paying other people to watch them grow up, and hoping to have a little bit of time with them on the weekends? Or, to learn a system to get 500 people to save money on their telephone bills?"

"So what is going to be easier for you? To continue going to work every day, hoping the boss will magically give you a 25% raise so that your children can go to private school? Or, to learn a system to help 200 families buy natural products for their homes instead of chemical products?"

"So what is going to be easier for you? To continue working hard every day until you are 65 years old, and then hope your health is good enough to enjoy your retirement? Or, to learn a system to get 200 people to use natural skincare products, so you can earn enough money to retire in three years?"

"So what is going to be easier for you? To continue waking up every morning to an alarm and dreading going to work? Or, to learn a system to help 45 people start their own part-time business by helping their neighbors save money on their utilities?"

"So what is going to be easier for you? To feel depressed every Sunday night because the weekend is over? Or, to learn a system to accumulate 300 families who would like to book their holidays through you?"

"So what is going to be easier for you? To spend your entire life working at a job you hate? Or, to learn a system to get 200 families to change their buying habits?"

"So what is going to be easier for you? To go back to school for four years and get that accounting degree so you can get a raise? Or, to learn a system to introduce our nutrition programs to seven people every week?"

PUTTING THE
PIECES TOGETHER.

Okay, we have all the pieces. Let's put it together and create a full two-minute story presentation. In the example below, we've added a simple summary after each sentence to remind us what we have learned so far.

The story.

I've got a good story. (We have their attention.)

Takes about two minutes. (It is short. They want to hear it now.)

It might make you a lot of money, might not. (Money? We have their interest. Might not? We increased their interest.)

Want to hear it? (Of course. Right now.)

Would it be okay if you never had to go to work again? (We triggered their dreams.)

So how much money would it take so that you would never have to show up for work again? (We get their minimum monthly expenses. We will use that later to describe what they would have to do to earn that money. In this example, our prospect told us that $5,000 covers the bills.)

Well, you know how people would love to have a lawyer to threaten the landlord, get even with the dry cleaners, get a refund from the mechanic, and fix those stupid speeding tickets they gave us by mistake? (Our prospects think, "Yeah. This is something everyone needs.")

Well, there is a company called Incredible-Lawyer-by-Telephone that does this service for only $30 a month. (Now they know what our company does.)

Now, if you never wanted to go to work again, all you would have to do is let people know about this benefit, and eventually accumulate 500 individuals who use the service. (They see themselves talking to a group of employees in the lunchroom. But, 500 sounds like a lot of people.)

Now, you don't know how to get 500 people to use our service, but you can learn. (The prospect feels a lot better, knowing that we understand this sounds hard to do.)

You learned how to drive a car, you learned how to use your laptop, and you certainly can learn a system to talk to a few people a day until you have 500 people using our service. (System? They think, "Sure, I can learn.")

And then you would earn an extra $5,000 a month. (We remind them of their original dream.)

So what is going to be easier for you? (We are kind to prospects. We make it easy. They only have two choices.)

To continue going to work with your long commute, and missing out on your children's activities? (Life as it is.)

Or, to learn a system to help 500 people use our legal service? (Or choose our solution.)

Pretty clear.

In less than two minutes, our prospect gets the picture. Even if he has no idea about legal services and how they work, he can make a decision. He can keep his life the same. Or, he can learn a system to talk to people about the legal services.

Prospects can make a "yes" or "no" decision now. And if the answer is "yes" to this story, then they can learn all the details in training.

Can we change the story?

Each sentence works hard and helps our prospects make an easy final decision. The two-minute story is all about making the process easy for our prospects. The two-minute story is short and saves time for our prospects, while providing the important points necessary for our prospects' decision.

Our natural temptation is to provide more information to our prospects. We do this based upon the misguided belief that prospects make decisions based on information. If you have read our book on *Pre-Closing*, you know this isn't true. Prospects make their decisions before the details. Too much information confuses our prospects.

Think of it this way. Our prospects can't understand our business right away. They don't know how to work our business. And, they don't even know the right questions to ask.

The only real decision our prospects can make is, "Do I want to be in business with you, or not?" They have to learn, no matter which business they choose. That is why it is difficult for them to make a decision about any business.

However, it is easy for them to make a decision if they want to be in business with us or not.

That is why our two-minute story concentrates on the decision, "Do I want to learn a system with you, or not?" Our two-minute story is not about our company's information. That information will come later in training if they decide to join.

So, let's take a look at a variety of two-minute stories in the next chapter. Once we are familiar with the pattern of these stories, we can design our own two-minute story.

Most of these stories will take slightly longer than one minute. Our prospects will be thrilled with how little time our story takes.

Want one more benefit to using the two-minute story?

Our prospects realize that they can duplicate our success by learning a simple two-minute story. Compare that to what prospects think after hearing a 45-minute presentation.

They think, "Oh, I could never do that. 45 minutes of information is too much to memorize. None of my friends would sit through a 45-minute commercial."

There are many more benefits to the two-minute story. You will discover them as you use the two-minute story presentation in your business.

Some two-minute story presentations.

Use these examples as templates to create our own two-minute story presentation. Once we design our own two-minute story, we will want to use it as often as possible. It's easy for us, and easy on our prospects.

Natural cleaners.

I've got a good story. Takes about two minutes. It might make you a lot of money, might not. Want to hear it?

Would it be okay if you never had to go to work again? So how much money would it take so that you would never have to show up for work again?

Well, you know how people worry about our environment and always want to help? Well, there is a company called Super Natural Cleaners that makes natural cleaning products to replace all those chemical cleaners we have around our houses.

Now, if you never wanted to go to work again, all you would have to do is tell families they now have a natural choice for their cleaning products, and eventually get 250 families to use the new natural cleaning products.

Now, you don't know how to get 250 families to use the natural cleaning products, but you can learn. You learned how to drive a car, you learned how to use your smartphone, and you certainly can learn a system to get 250 families to change their cleaning products. And then you would earn an extra $5,000 a month.

So what is going to be easier for you? To continue going to that job you have no passion for, or to learn a system to help families improve our environment and have a career with meaning?

Vitamins and energy drinks.

I've got a good story. Takes about two minutes. It might make you a lot of money, might not. Want to hear it?

Would it be okay if you never had to go to work again? So how much money would it take so that you would never have to show up for work again?

Well, you know how most people are taking handfuls of vitamins and buying energy drinks every day? Well, there is a company called Awesome Healthy Wonderful Products that makes cool versions of healthy products and an all-natural, super-organic energy drink people love.

Now, if you never wanted to go to work again, all you would have to do is get people to sample these products every day until you get 300 people who order their healthy products from you regularly.

Now, you don't know how to get 300 people hooked on these healthy products, but you can learn. You learned how to use the Internet, you learned how to speak Spanish, and you certainly can learn a system to get 300 people to use these products. And then you would earn an extra $5,000 a month.

So what is going to be easier for you? To continue commuting two hours every day to work, or to learn our sampling system to so that you can work out of your home instead?

Utilities.

I've got a good story. Takes about two minutes. It might make you a lot of money, might not. Want to hear it?

Would it be okay if you never had to go to work again? So how much money would it take so that you would never have to show up for work again?

Well, you know how everyone gets electricity bills, phone bills, and other utility bills? Well, there is a company called Pay-Us-Less that makes those bills smaller, so people have more money in their pockets.

Now, if you never wanted to go to work again, all you would have to do is build a team of 40 part-time neighborhood helpers and teach them how to get their neighbors to receive lower utility bills.

Now, you don't know how to build a team of 40 part-time neighborhood helpers, but you can learn. You learned how to organize our volunteer club, you learned how to run our parents' group, and you certainly can learn a system to get 40 part-time neighborhood helpers. And then you would earn an extra $5,000 a month.

So what is going to be easier for you? To continue balancing two jobs and a family, or to learn our system to build neighborhood helpers so that you never have to go to your jobs again?

Travel.

I've got a good story. Takes about two minutes. It might make you a lot of money, might not. Want to hear it?

Would it be okay if you never had to go to work again? So how much money would it take so that you would never have to show up for work again?

Well, you know how people love taking holidays and forgetting about their jobs for two weeks? Well, there is a company called Cheap-But-Stylish-Travel that helps us get huge discounts so we can take five-star holidays for the price of staying at a cheap hotel.

Now, if you never wanted to go to work again, all you would have to do is get 300 families to save money by switching from their boring holidays to Cheap-But-Stylish-Travel's luxury all-inclusive holidays.

Now, you don't know how to locate 300 families who want to switch to better holidays, but you can learn. You learned how to become an accountant, you learned how to get a driver's license, and you certainly can learn a system to help 300 families save money while getting better holidays. And then you would earn an extra $5,000 a month.

So what is going to be easier for you? To continue working that accounting job and helping your boss get rich, or to learn a system to help 300 families save money and have holidays that they will remember forever?

Diet products.

I've got a good story. Takes about two minutes. It might make you a lot of money, might not. Want to hear it?

Would it be okay if you never had to go to work again? So how much money would it take so that you would never have to show up for work again?

Well, you know how people are always exercising, starving themselves, and watching their weight come back? Well, there is a company called Thinner-Breakfast that makes a delicious chocolate breakfast drink that helps people lose weight one time, and keep it off forever.

Now, if you never wanted to go to work again, all you would have to do is find 200 struggling dieters who are tired of dieting, and want their breakfast to keep them fit for life.

Now, you don't know how to find 200 struggling dieters, but you can learn. You learned how to find the local donut shop, and you learned how to avoid health clubs and exercise, and you certainly can learn a system to locate 200 struggling dieters who want to lose weight one time and keep it off forever. And then you would earn an extra $5,000 a month.

So what is going to be easier for you? To continue hoping your boss will give you a 200% raise, or to learn a system to help struggling dieters lose weight, and never have to beg for a raise again?

Cosmetics.

I've got a good story. Takes about two minutes. It might make you a lot of money, might not. Want to hear it?

Would it be okay if you never had to go to work again? So how much money would it take so that you would never have to show up for work again?

Well, you know how women love to buy cosmetics to look great? Well, there is a company called Newer-Than-New Cosmetics that manufactures all-natural cosmetics that make faces glow.

Now, if you never wanted to go to work again, all you would have to do is pass out enough samples of our magic foundation to find 300 women who want to look better every day of their lives.

Now, you don't know where to find these women, or how to get them to try the foundation sample, but you can learn. You learned how to dance, you learned how to organize our women's group, and you certainly can learn a system to find 300 women who want to look better every day of their lives. And then you would earn an extra $5,000 a month.

So what is going to be easier for you? To continue working for that tiny paycheck from our dream-sucking boss, or to learn a system to pass out enough foundation samples so that we never have to show up to this low-paying job again?

See a pattern yet?

It should be easy to create our own two-minute story from the above examples. The two-minute story is easy to learn and easy to tell.

Why does the two-minute story seem so natural?

Our minds want to make a decision first, and learn the details later. The two-minute story helps our prospects make a "yes" or "no" decision quickly.

If our prospect's decision is "no," we simply talk about something else.

If our prospect's decision is "yes," then going into more detail makes sense.

WHY THIS WORKS.

Why does our two-minute story connect so well with prospects?

Bill Jayne says it best. He tells marketers, "It doesn't matter what you are selling. Your direct marketing should never be about the product. It should always be about the prospect."

That is the secret. Our two-minute story is all about our prospects. They love it. We love it. It saves everyone time, but ...

We can't use it all the time.

Imagine an opportunity meeting at the local hotel. The two-minute story would not be appropriate for a presentation.

The first problem? We couldn't ask everyone for their minimum monthly expenses. Some guests may only need $3,000 a month. Other guests might need a lot more.

Second problem? Our entire presentation would be over in two minutes. Our guests drove all the way to our meeting ... and it only lasted two minutes? There will be some unhappy guests.

Third problem? What about a presentation to a detail-addicted accountant? The two-minute story wouldn't be an adequate explanation.

But most of the time, our one-on-one or two-on-one presentations can use the two-minute story effectively. We may also find it to be a perfect solution for many phone conversations.

The two-minute story should be used when appropriate. There are many other presentation methods available. As professionals, we should evaluate the situation and decide which method is appropriate at the time.

One last reminder.

Remember that all the examples in this book are for $5,000 a month. We can create a two-minute story for any amount of monthly income.

WHERE CAN WE USE OUR TWO-MINUTE STORY?

The possibilities are endless. Most presentations take a long time or require a special business setting. Our short and flexible two-minute story presentation can fit into almost any conversation. Here are some examples.

Use our two-minute story with cold prospects.

Imagine we sent our cold prospect to look at a video on our website. Our follow-up call might go something like this.

Us: Just checking back to see if you had a chance to look at the video. If you are like most people, you haven't had a chance to look at it yet. (The prospect relaxes and thinks, "You are a mind-reader!" Now we have great rapport with our prospect.)

Prospect: Yes, you are right. I did not get a chance to look at the video yet.

Us: No problem. I know you are busy. I will get back to you in a week or so. (Prospect relaxes even more.)

Prospect: Thanks.

Us: Oh, and one more thing. I've got a good story. Takes about two minutes. Might make you a lot of money, might not. Want to hear it?

Prospect: Yes! (We turned off the salesman alarm, and now our prospect eagerly waits for our story.)

Use our two-minute story during coffee break.

Everyone looks for new and refreshing conversation during coffee breaks. All we have to say to our co-workers is, "I've got a good story." The conversation and story are easy.

Use our two-minute story at family reunions.

What should we say when a relative asks us, "What is new with you?"

Easy. We simply reply, "I've got a good story." Everyone wants to listen to a story.

Use our two-minute story at networking events.

What should we say when someone asks us, "What do you do for a living?"

Easy. We simply reply, "I've got a good story." This already sounds interesting to our conversation partner.

WHAT COULD HAPPEN.

Most of us can't wait to tell our two-minute story several times a day. Let's look at the possibilities.

Three times a day.

Imagine we set a personal goal to tell our two-minute story three times a day. Anyone can fit that into a schedule. For some people, they could do this while commuting. Others could tell their stories at work. Many will tell their stories while chatting with their friends.

If we succeed in telling our two-minute story three times a day, that means 90 prospects hear our story every month! That's 90 people who hear how they never have to show up to work again.

So out of the 90 prospects who hear our story, how many will want to join us and our opportunity?

Even if we are bad, really bad, and we ruin 90% of the prospects we talk to ... that still leaves us with nine new personally-sponsored distributors. And this assumes incompetence. Out of 90 people, we surely would have nine volunteers no matter how badly we messed up.

The good news about a two-minute story is that prospects love stories that are short and to the point. A terrible two-minute story is always better than a perfect one-hour presentation.

But what if we are good, really good, with our two-minute story presentation? Then, almost everyone will want to join. If the timing is right for our prospects, our two-minute story is the most exciting news they can imagine. "Never have to go to work again" is a dream come true.

Are we seeing an expressway to success?

But what if my prospect isn't interested in my story?

Move on. There is an old saying, "No matter how hard we dance, some people ain't going to clap."

If our prospect isn't interested, we change the subject and talk about something else. That is how most conversations work. We will eventually find something that is interesting for both of us to talk about.

This is so good, we want our team to use it too.

So our next step is to get some serious team members to commit to telling their two-minute story at least once a day.

What to say to team members.

Now, here is a strategy. Explain our two-minute story plan to members on our team. Here is an example of what we could say.

Every day, tell ONE person this little two-minute story presentation. Say, "I've got a good story. Takes about two minutes. Might make you a lot of money, might not. Want to hear it?"

Then, we will tell our two-minute story.

That is it!

No need to close. No need to harass. No need to follow up. Our prospects either "get it" or they "don't get it."

Now, if some of our prospects "don't get it," we don't want to pressure them into joining our business. If we force them to join, we will have to sell them over and over again, every day. Now we become a full-time babysitter, re-convincing these new team members each day. We hate it. They hate it. They become "vampire team members" because they suck the life out of us daily. They want us to buy their products, sell their products, find their people, train their people, listen to their personal problems, and they will blame us, our company, and anyone they can think of, for every bad thing that happens in their lives.

If some of our prospects are skeptical, leave them alone. Skeptics make terrible entrepreneurs. They look for reasons to sabotage their success. They spend their energy looking for reasons why it won't work for them. To be a successful entrepreneur, these skeptics need counseling. We are not qualified as counselors.

Yes, the skeptics are happy finding reasons why things won't work. Leave them alone. If we waste time counseling the skeptics, we will miss the good people who will happily build our business.

Now, if some of our prospects "get it," they will say, "So how can I get started?"

Consider this a leadership test. They pass. We love these people. They will always be looking for reasons why their business will work.

Now if we tell this little story 365 times this year, some people will join. These are the people we want. So, don't tell the story with an agenda, don't try to manipulate people to join. Simply tell the story, take the volunteers that "get it" … and we will never experience rejection.

Tell this story 30 times this month, lean back, take the volunteers that "get it." Work with them, show them how to tell the story. Repeat.

But I know we want to enhance the story. We want more people to volunteer to join.

In that case, we could say this to our favorite people:

"I am telling this story once a day. I will become a Diamond in about six months. It will be fun. It will change my life. You know, six months from now is going to come anyway. I might as well have $5,000 a month coming in. I look forward to the trips, the extra cash, and spending more time with my friends and relatives who decided to come along with me too."

Most people are followers. They desperately try to find someone to lead them. When we state that we are going to become a Diamond "with them or without them," many people are going to say,

"Hey, take me with you. I don't like where I am going, I like where you are going."

Now we are attracting people.

This is different than hard-selling or begging people. Desperation drives people away.

Not having an agenda is better. We should think like this:

"Hey, I will tell you this two-minute story. I don't mind if you join or not. That is up to you. I just tell the story, and if it is the right time in your life, you will jump at the opportunity. If it is not the right time in your life, then you might remember the story when the timing is better for you. My job is to tell the story and take the volunteers."

I know we can tell this story once a day. We don't want to be salespeople. We don't want to beg. We don't want to babysit people.

Next, everyone has 20 seconds to tell others something good that happened to them during the week. Of course, plenty of bad things happen. But this is not the forum for bad things. We only talk about the good things that happen. This gives the other participants a feeling that good things can happen in their business. When we hear about good things happening, we build a belief of hope and expectation that even though this week was bad, next week could be better.

Next, one person demonstrates their two-minute story presentation. This takes less than two minutes. The other members of the group can compliment and make suggestions. Each week, a different person gives their two-minute story presentation.

The call leader compliments everyone for their efforts that week and challenges them to do seven more two-minute story presentations the following week. (Or four, or five, or whatever goal or standard you set for this group.)

And finally, a word of motivation. The leader might say something like:

"I absolutely know you will all get to Executive Director. I just don't know how fast. But you are definitely on your way."

Or, "You don't know what will happen next week. One person you speak with might earn you $20,000. They just have to hear your story."

Or, "Our job is to give people a chance to have the life of their dreams. Our obligation is to give them the chance. The rest is up to them."

And now our weekly call is over.

Let's invite our selected team members now. Here is a sample of what we might say:

Instructions for the call.

"Hi, everyone.

"Let's start things off right during our first call on Thursday night.

"On our weekly group calls, our introduction should be something like this:

"1. Hi, John Smith, here on the call. (Let us know that you are on the call.)

"2. I personally told my two-minute story three times this week. (This is our basic weekly goal. We tell our story to our prospects.)

"3. My group told the two-minute story 13 times this week. (The more people that hear our opportunity, the more volunteers we will have on our team.)

"4. Here is something good that has happened in my business this week. (Discouraging things happen. This call is not about discouraging events. We should reinforce that good things happen too. Everyone on the call will feel better and more confident when we hear that good things happened this week.)

"These four items should take less than 30 seconds for each one of us. We limit our group to eight people so that our weekly calls will be short.

"Then, one of us will give our personal two-minute story for the rest of the team members on the call to hear. We will then offer any suggestions that come to mind for this two-minute story presentation.

"Next, we will learn some more tips about the two-minute story so that we can tell it more often.

"We finish up with any questions. In 20 minutes or less, our weekly coaching call is over.

"That is it!

"Now, what can you do between now and our first Thursday call?

"1. Stop by my webpage and read my two-minute story presentation.

"2. Memorize the two-minute story so it will sound more natural.

"3. Try telling the two-minute story for a bit of experience. Maybe you will have something to report on our very first call. That would be great.

"Looking forward to Thursday evening's call."

How to sponsor new team members who will join our weekly calls.

Leverage!

Scale up!

Duplication!

Yes, we can tell our two-minute story several times a day. But, we only have 24 hours in a day. To create massive growth on our team, we need new people who can present the two-minute story.

The more people that join our weekly training calls, the more guaranteed presentations we will have.

Leverage? Absolutely! We will multiply our success through the efforts of other people.

Where are we going to find these special people?

Our strategy.

"Blue" personalities love to talk. They are natural-born storytellers. They live to talk. They live to tell stories. And, they love to tell stories to new people.

Does this sound like a match?

"What would you like to DO next?"

Easy.

Our prospects made a decision to join our business a long time ago. If their original answer was "No," then we would not be this far into our conversation. All we want to know now is what they would like to do next.

Prospects love this question. We acknowledge that they control the decisions in their lives.

Their choices? Only two.

#1. To continue their lives as they are.

#2. To join with us and change their lives.

Sound familiar? It should.

Our prospects already made a decision to change their lives by talking to us now.

Closing? Getting a decision? That happened a long time ago. Now we want to know what they want to do next. Here are the most common responses we could expect:

- "Okay, let's start."

- "Sounds good. Can I use a credit card?"

- "I want to join. But I don't get paid until Friday. Can I join on Friday?"

- "I need to think it over." (We know this is a decision to stay where they are.)

- "Nothing good ever happens to me. I am a full-time loser. I know I will mess up. Let me save myself from the embarrassment of failure. I don't want to join." (We grant their wish.)

That's it. The rest is up to us.

When appropriate, we can choose to use our two-minute story instead of a long, boring presentation. Our prospects love it. We love it. And, in two minutes we can change someone's life … and our business too.

There are three types of people in the world.

1. Those who do not know how to tell a two-minute story for their business.

2. Those who know how to tell a two-minute story for their business, and don't use it.

3. Those who know how to tell a two-minute story for their business and use it to build a massive network marketing business.

Great skills work best when we use them.

MORE BIG AL BOOKS
BIGALBOOKS.COM

How to Build Your Network Marketing Business in 15 Minutes a Day

Anyone can set aside 15 minutes a day to start building their financial freedom. Of course we would like to have more time, but in just 15 minutes we can change our lives forever.

How to Meet New People Guidebook
Overcome Fear and Connect Now

Meeting new people is easy when we can read their minds. Discover how strangers automatically size us up in seconds, using three basic standards.

Why Are My Goals Not Working?
Color Personalities for Network Marketing Success

Setting goals that work for us is easy when we have guidelines and a checklist.

Closing for Network Marketing
Getting Prospects Across The Finish Line

Here are 46 years' worth of our best closes. All of these closes are kind and comfortable for prospects, and rejection-free for us.

Pre-Closing for Network Marketing
"Yes" Decisions Before The Presentation

Instead of selling to customers with facts, features and benefits, let's talk to prospects in a way they like. We can now get that "yes" decision first, so the rest of our presentation will be easy.

The One-Minute Presentation
Explain Your Network Marketing Business Like A Pro

Learn to make your business grow with this efficient, focused business presentation technique.

Retail Sales for Network Marketers
How to Get New Customers for Your MLM Business

Learn how to position your retail sales so people are happy to buy. Don't know where to find customers for your products and services? Learn how to market to people who want what you offer.

Getting "Yes" Decisions
What insurance agents and financial advisors can say to clients

In the new world of instant decisions, we need to master the words and phrases to successfully move our potential clients to lifelong clients. Easy … when we can read their minds and service their needs immediately.

3 Easy Habits For Network Marketing
Automate Your MLM Success

Use these habits to create a powerful stream of activity in your network marketing business.

Start SuperNetworking!
5 Simple Steps to Creating Your Own Personal Networking Group

Start your own personal networking group and have new, pre-sold customer and prospects come to you.

The Four Color Personalities for MLM
The Secret Language for Network Marketing

Learn the skill to quickly recognize the four personalities and how to use magic words to translate your message.

Ice Breakers!
How To Get Any Prospect To Beg You For A Presentation

Create unlimited Ice Breakers on-demand. Your distributors will no longer be afraid of prospecting, instead, they will love prospecting.

How To Get Instant Trust, Belief, Influence and Rapport!
13 Ways To Create Open Minds By Talking To The Subconscious Mind

Learn how the pros get instant rapport and cooperation with even the coldest prospects. The #1 skill every new distributor needs.

First Sentences for Network Marketing
How To Quickly Get Prospects On Your Side

Attract more prospects and give more presentations with great first sentences that work.

Motivation. Action. Results.
How Network Marketing Leaders Move Their Teams

Learn the motivational values and triggers our team members have, and learn to use them wisely. By balancing internal motivation and external motivation methods, we can be more effective motivators.

How To Build Network Marketing Leaders
Volume One: Step-By-Step Creation Of MLM Professionals

This book will give you the step-by-step activities to actually create leaders.

How To Build Network Marketing Leaders
Volume Two: Activities And Lessons For MLM Leaders

You will find many ways to change people's viewpoints, to change their beliefs, and to reprogram their actions.

The Complete Three-Book Network Marketing Leadership Series

Series includes: How To Build Network Marketing Leaders Volume One, How To Build Network Marketing Leaders Volume Two, and Motivation. Action. Results.

51 Ways and Places to Sponsor New Distributors
Discover Hot Prospects For Your Network Marketing Business

Learn the best places to find motivated people to build your team and your customer base.

How to Follow Up With Your Network Marketing Prospects
Turn Not Now Into Right Now!

Use the techniques in this book to move your prospects forward from "Not Now" to "Right Now!"

How To Prospect, Sell And Build Your Network Marketing Business With Stories

If you want to communicate effectively, add your stories to deliver your message.

26 Instant Marketing Ideas To Build Your Network Marketing Business

176 pages of amazing marketing lessons and case studies to get more prospects for your business immediately.

Big Al's MLM Sponsoring Magic
How To Build A Network Marketing Team Quickly

This book shows the beginner exactly what to do, exactly what to say, and does it through the eyes of a brand-new distributor.

Public Speaking Magic

Success and Confidence in the First 20 Seconds

By using any of the three major openings in this book, we can confidently start our speeches and presentations without fear.

Worthless Sponsor Jokes

Network Marketing Humor

Here is a collection of worthless sponsor jokes from 25 years of the "Big Al Report." Network marketing can be enjoyable, and we can have fun making jokes along the way.

How To Get Kids To Say Yes!

Using the Secret Four Color Languages to Get Kids to Listen

Turn discipline and frustration into instant cooperation. Kids love to say "yes" when they hear their own color-coded language.

ABOUT THE AUTHORS

Keith Schreiter has 20+ years of experience in network marketing and MLM. He shows network marketers how to use simple systems to build a stable and growing business.

So, do you need more prospects? Do you need your prospects to commit instead of stalling? Want to know how to engage and keep your group active? If these are the types of skills you would like to master, you will enjoy his "how-to" style.

Keith speaks and trains in the U.S., Canada, and Europe.

Tom "Big Al" Schreiter has 40+ years of experience in network marketing and MLM. As the author of the original "Big Al" training books in the late '70s, he has continued to speak in over 80 countries on using the exact words and phrases to get prospects to open up their minds and say "YES."

His passion is marketing ideas, marketing campaigns, and how to speak to the subconscious mind in simplified, practical ways. He is always looking for case studies of incredible marketing campaigns that give usable lessons.

As the author of numerous audio trainings, Tom is a favorite speaker at company conventions and regional events.